PYTHON

PAULINE REILLY

Illustrated by
WILL ROLLAND

KANGAROO PRESS

We acknowledge with thanks the assistance
and advice of Professor Richard Shine.
He suggested this book because he loves snakes
and wrote about them in his book
Australian Snakes: A Natural History.

© Pauline Reilly (text) and Will Rolland (illustrations) 1995

First published in 1995 by Kangaroo Press Pty. Ltd.
3 Whitehall Road Kenthurst NSW 2156 Australia
PO Box 6125 Dural Delivery Centre NSW 2158
Printed in Singapore by Kyodo Printing Co (S'pore) Pte Ltd

ISBN 0 86417 698 8

In a nest near a stream in a valley,
Python pushed with the tiny egg tooth
on the end of her snout
and came out into the world.

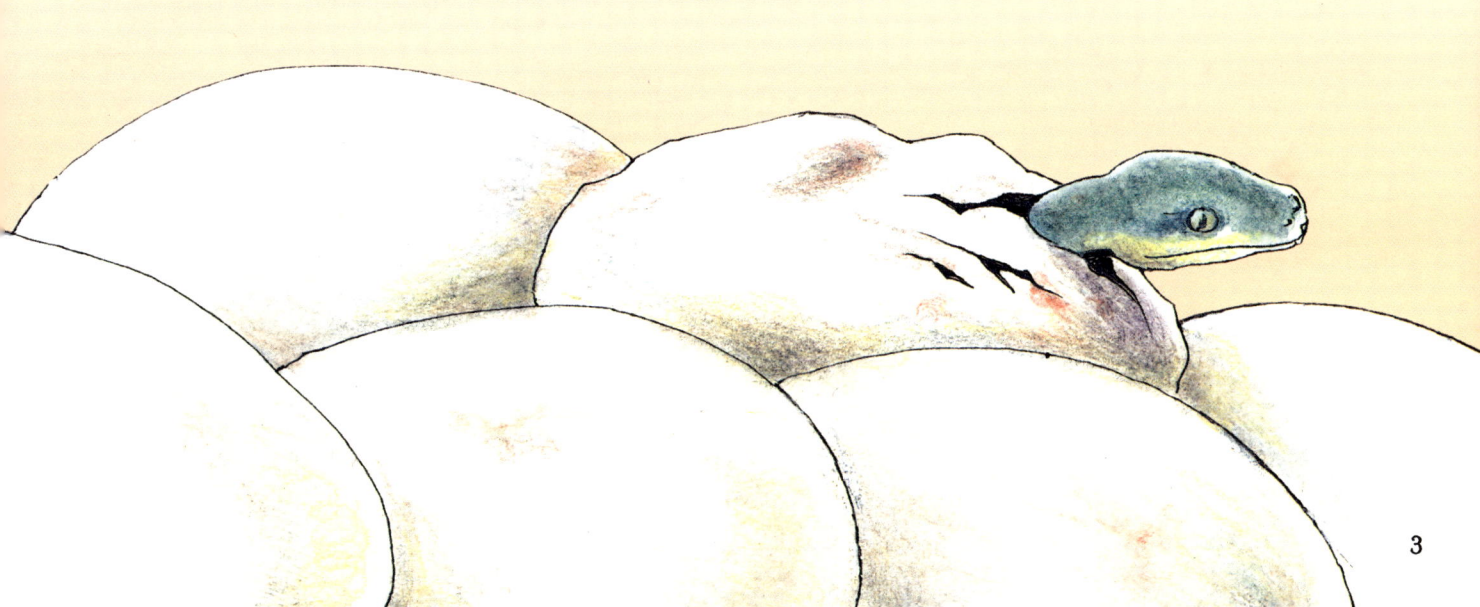

She saw her mother lying coiled
around some eggs and her siblings
fighting their way out of their soft leathery shells.

Python wriggled away from the nest
into the late summer sunshine.

4

Sometimes she pulled herself along the ground
like a caterpillar but more often she looped
her body from side to side and
pushed against the ground.

When she crossed a stream,
she used the same looping action
and pushed against the water.

By the end of her first week, Python had grown bigger
and her skin was too tight.
She pushed her head and snout against rocks
and branches until her old skin broke loose.

She kept pushing forward until
her old skin peeled back and lay inside out
on the ground.

At night she sheltered under some dead leaves.

In the morning,
she moved slowly into the sunshine.

As soon as she was warm,
she was ready to eat.
She flicked her forked tongue in and out,
tasting the air
for the warmth and smell of animals.
She could feel their movements
through the ground.

Python did not hunt. Instead, each day
she waited in ambush.
She was not easy to see,
curled up and not moving in the grass
near the scent trails of small animals.

She caught the animals in her mouth
and held them with her coiled body.

    Their bones did not break
    but they could not breathe. She swallowed them head first.

After eating, she basked in the sun.
Its warmth helped her to digest her prey.

When she was thirsty, she pushed
her snout into the water. Then she pumped
the water down her throat.

There was plenty of prey where Python lived
but she mostly ate lizards.
She was still too small to eat birds
and mice and possums, but she kept growing.

Each time her skin became too tight,
she sloughed it off, just as she had
when she was a baby.

Until she grew bigger, Python always hid
when kookaburras came near.
One had tried to pick her up
but she had escaped into a hollow log.

In the winter, Python found a crack
in a rocky cliff warmed by the sun.

She rested through most of the cold weather.
Because she rested, she did not need to eat
until she went back into the world in the springtime.

For two more winters, Python lived
inside the warm, dry roof of a house.
The owners of the house liked her to be there
because she caught the rats and mice
that sheltered from the cold.

When she was four years old,
Python moved into the woodlands.
She left a scent trail behind her.
It was spring and time for her to mate.

Three male pythons followed her scent trail ready
to mate with her. One male ran his head up and down her back
while she lay still. They mated.

Python left the male.

Down by the stream, she burrowed under some leaves to make a nest
and a month later, she laid her eggs.

The male would never see the eggs
or know his babies.

Python coiled her body around the eggs
to keep them warm. But her nest was too close to the stream.

When it flooded, her eggs washed away.

Two years later, Python was ready to mate again.
This time she nested in a safer place.
A goanna tried to steal her eggs but she fought it off
by hissing and pretending to strike.

By basking in the early morning sunshine
and shivering as she lay coiled around the eggs,
she kept them warm for three months.
As each baby python hatched, it went off into the world . . .

. . . and so the cycle of life continued.

DID YOU KNOW?

- The scientific name of the Diamond Python and the Carpet Python is *Morelia spilota* (Maw-reel´-ee-ah spy-lote´-ah). The meaning of *Morelia* is unknown but *spilota* means spotted.

- There are seven families of snakes in Australia: elapids (venomous), seasnakes, blindsnakes, pythons, colubrids (non-venomous), sea kraits and filesnakes.

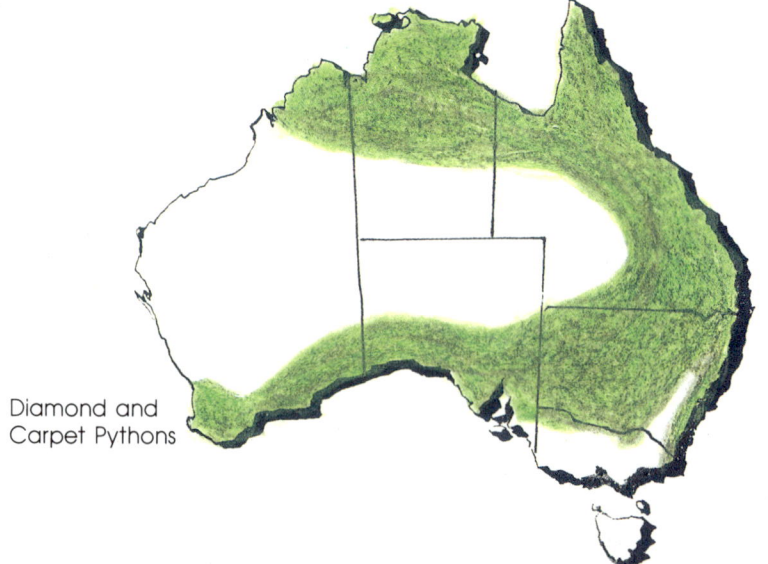

Diamond and
Carpet Pythons

- Snakes need the sun to warm them because their bodies are not warm like human bodies.

- Some snakes can travel at 10 kilometres an hour for a short distance but most are much slower.

- Pythons continue to grow throughout their lives. Females are larger than males.

- Females may lay up to 40 eggs in one clutch. The bigger they are, the more eggs they lay.

- A Diamond Python may grow to 180 centimetres, as big as a good-sized man. The biggest Australian snake is the Amethistine or Scrub Python at more than eight metres and the smallest is the blind snake at 12 centimetres.

- Australian pythons eat mostly mammals though some prefer reptiles. They are not venomous and they do not eat people, although some African and Asian pythons do occasionally eat people.

- A large python can swallow a small wallaby slowly by opening its mouth and disconnecting its jaws. It can also go without food for years.

- Pythons are most often seen in the spring. Males searching for females may travel up to a kilometre in one day. Male Diamond Pythons do not fight each other but Carpet Pythons and other snakes do.

- Pythons may live up to 40 years.

SNAKE or LIZARD?

ℒ Snakes are covered with scales, even their eyes, which cannot blink. The clear scale over the eye is shed with the skin.

ℒ Snakes do not see well, especially things that are not moving, nor do they hear well as they are without earholes, but they have a very strong sense of smell.

ℒ Lizards have ear holes and long tails and most of them blink but some, like geckos, do not. The goanna is the snake's closest relative. It is the only lizard with a forked tongue but you know it is not a snake because it has legs and it blinks.

THE INSIDE STORY

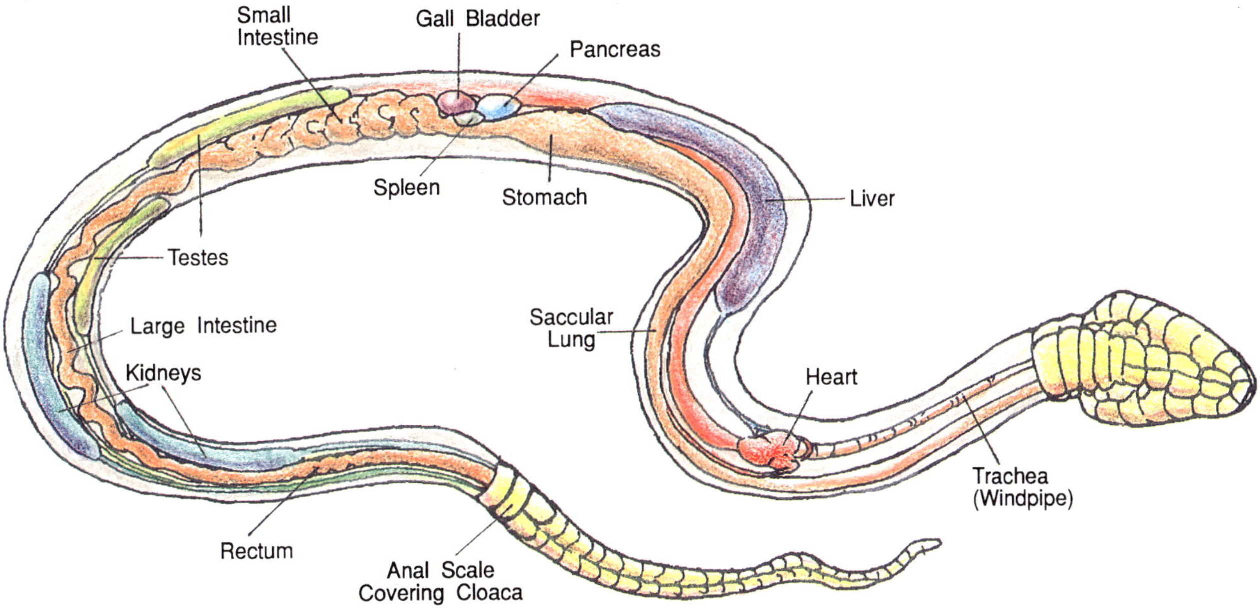

Small Intestine

Gall Bladder

Pancreas

Spleen

Stomach

Liver

Testes

Saccular Lung

Heart

Large Intestine

Kidneys

Trachea (Windpipe)

Rectum

Anal Scale Covering Cloaca

ℒ The bodies of snakes are like stretched-out human bodies without arms and legs.

ℒ The human spine has 32 bones (vertebrae). Some snakes have up to 400.

29

LIVING WITH SNAKES

There are some silly ideas about snakes that are not true. They do not milk cows or put their tails in their mouths and roll downhill like a hoop and pythons do not breed with taipans to produce enormous dangerous snakes.

All snakes are useful to humans. They stay in the same place for a long time and are ready to eat up plagues of rats and mice.

Watch where you tread. Snakes don't like to be trodden on any more than you do.

Around your home, keep the grass short and clear of hiding places. Snakes don't like to cross open spaces.

Snakes strike at their victims for two reasons: hunger and fear. If humans leave them alone, they glide away. If they can't escape, they threaten by hissing and trying to look larger.

Hundreds of people claim they are bitten by snakes each year in Australia, usually when they try to kill or catch them. Only about five of the bitten die.

If you are bitten, DON'T PANIC. Snakes don't always inject venom. Bites are usually on arms and legs. Bandage the limb firmly, keep it raised and still, identify the snake if you can and go to a doctor. It may takes hours or even days before there is damage, if any.

Snakes have their enemies: cats, dogs, foxes, cane toads and people. Don't run over snakes or kill them. They are protected in Australia. If you want one removed, contact the government Conservation Department for the name of the nearest snake catcher.

Snakes are part of our heritage just like kangaroos and koalas and penguins. We need to preserve their habitat as we do for all other animals.

People are not better than other animals, including snakes. Snakes are not inferior to people. They are just different.

Children are wrongly taught in story books to hate and fear snakes as something evil. Learn about snakes and fear will go.

LEARN ABOUT SNAKES AND FEAR WILL GO.